Forest Trees

By Sally Cowan

Illustrations by Andrew Louey

T0342754

Contents

Discovery of a Giant Tree

A giant tree was recently discovered in a forest in Tasmania, Australia. The tree is a swamp gum, which is a type of evergreen gum tree. It is believed to be the tallest flowering plant on Earth.

Swamp gums are only found in cool, wet forests in small areas of Australia.

3

The giant tree is 101 metres tall. It might once have been even taller, because the top of the tree was broken off at some time in the past. It then re-sprouted to its present height. Forestry workers named the tree "Centurion". A centurion was an ancient Roman officer in charge of 100 soldiers. The workers thought it was a suitable name for a tree just over 100 metres tall.

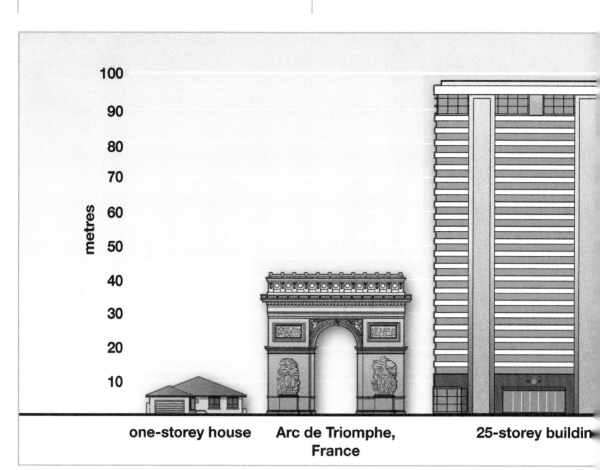

one-storey house   Arc de Triomphe, France   25-storey buildin

180

170

160

150

140

130

120

110

Centurion

**Great Pyramid of Giza,
Egypt**

At the base of the tree, the huge trunk is very wide. It has a diameter of four metres. The bark at the base of the trunk is dark and rough.

Several metres up, the bark peels away to reveal a pale grey, smooth trunk.

diameter 4 metres

The tall, straight tree trunk gets narrower as it rises. Short branches grow all around the treetop. These branches have clumps of long, thin leaves.

Centurion is about 400 years old. Next to it stands another swamp gum giant of 86.5 metres, called Triarius.

In the future, there may not be many giant trees left. Because trees less than 85 metres tall are not considered giant trees, they are not protected and can be cut down. These trees are chopped up to make different wood products, such as furniture and paper.

Centurion

Triarius

HOW TREES GROW IN A FOREST

Some forests have many different types of trees, while others have just a few.

Most trees grow in the following way. First, a seed falls from a tree and lands on the forest floor. The seed may stay there for months, or even years, without growing.

When a seed gets enough light, warmth and water, it will split and begin to grow.

The shoot grows up towards the light, and its roots grow down into the ground.

The roots feed the plant with water and nutrients from the soil.

seed

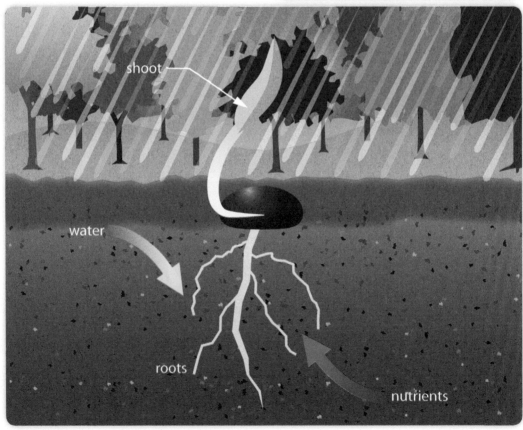

shoot

water

roots

nutrients

Next, the shoot grows leaves. The leaves absorb sunlight. They use energy from sunlight, air and water to make food for the plant. The leaves use some of the food and the rest goes into the stem and the roots.

The young tree grows branches with many leaves to absorb as much sunlight as possible.

Other plants and trees may be growing near the young tree. It has to compete with them for sunlight. If the tree is in shade, it may not grow straight up. It will gently bend towards a place where it can get the most sunlight.

As the tree grows, the trunk gets thicker and the roots spread. The roots grow stronger to hold the tree in place.

In a forest, different trees grow to different sizes. This will depend on the type of tree and the area in which it grows. But all forest trees have the same needs: sunlight, air and water.